Dinesh Gupta

Strategic allocation of resources using linear programming model with parametric analysis

in MATLAB and Excel Solver

Anchor Academic
Publishing

Gupta, Dinesh: Strategic allocation of resources using linear programming model with parametric analysis: in MATLAB and Excel Solver. Hamburg, Anchor Academic Publishing 2014

Buch-ISBN: 978-3-95489-280-8
PDF-eBook-ISBN: 978-3-95489-780-3
Druck/Herstellung: Anchor Academic Publishing, Hamburg, 2014

Bibliografische Information der Deutschen Nationalbibliothek:
Die Deutsche Nationalbibliothek verzeichnet diese Publikation in der Deutschen Nationalbibliografie; detaillierte bibliografische Daten sind im Internet über http://dnb.d-nb.de abrufbar.

Bibliographical Information of the German National Library:
The German National Library lists this publication in the German National Bibliography. Detailed bibliographic data can be found at: http://dnb.d-nb.de

© Anchor Academic Publishing, Imprint der Diplomica Verlag GmbH
Hermannstal 119k, 22119 Hamburg
http://www.diplomica-verlag.de, Hamburg 2014
Printed in Germany

ABSTRACT

Since the late 1940s, linear programming models have been used for many different purposes. Airline companies apply these models to optimize their use of planes and staff. NASA has been using them for many years to optimize their use of limited resources. Oil companies use them to optimize their refinery operations. Small and medium-sized businesses use linear programming to solve a huge variety of problems, often involving resource allocation.

In my study, a typical product-mix problem in a manufacturing system producing two products (each product consists of two sub-assemblies) is solved for its optimal solution through the use of the latest versions of MATLAB having the command *simlp*, which is very much like *linprog*. As analysts, we try to find a good enough solution for the decision maker to make a final decision. Our attempt is to give the mathematical description of the product-mix optimization problem and bring the problem into a form ready to call MATLAB's *simlp* command. The objective of this paper is to find the best product mix that maximizes profit. The graph obtained using MATLAB commands, give the shaded area enclosed by the constraints called the feasible region, which is the set of points satisfying all the constraints. To find the optimal solution we look at the lines of equal profit to find the corner of the feasible region which yield the highest profit. This corner can be found out at the farthest line of equal profit which still touches the feasible region.

The most critical part is the sensitivity analysis using Excel Solver and Parametric Analysis using computer software which allows us to study the effect on optimal solution due to discrete and continuous change in parameters of the LP model including to identify bottlenecks. We have examined other options like product outsourcing, one-time cost, cross training of one operator, manufacturing of hypothetical third product on under-utilized machines and optimal sequencing of jobs on machines.

ACKNOWLEDGEMENT

First and foremost, I thank the almighty God and my dear parents for being with me throughout this work.

I wish to express my deep sense of gratitude and sincere thanks to Dr. Anish Sachdeva, Associate Professor, Department of Industrial and Production Engineering, National Institute of Technology, Jalandhar, who has been a constant source of encouragement for me throughout my work. This work is simply the reflection of his thoughts, ideas, and concepts and above all his efforts. I have been fortunate to work under his supervision.

I would like to express my heartfelt gratitude to Dr. Ajay Gupta , Associate Professor, Department of Industrial and Production Engineering, National Institute of Technology, Jalandhar, for his invaluable professional guidance, continuous encouragement, valuable suggestions and inspiration throughout my course of study.

I would also like to thank all my friends for the timely help, advice and suggestions, which contributed directly or indirectly to the success of this work.

Flt Lt Dinesh Kumar Gupta

Dedicated

to

My Mother and Father

who let me make my own decisions and showed me how to live with integrity.

TABLE OF CONTENTS

CHAPTER 5
RESULT & DISCUSSIONS

CHAPTER 6
CONCLUSIONS

LIST OF FIGURES

LIST OF TABLES

LIST OF ABBREVIATIONS

Abbreviation	Expansion
GAMS	General Algebraic Modeling System
INF	Infinity
LP	Linear Programming
OE	Operating Expenses
OFC	Objective Function Coefficient
OR	Operation Research
POM	Production and Operations Management
RM	Raw Material
TOC	Theory of Constraints

CHAPTER 1
INTRODUCTION

1.1 HISTORY

Linear programming was developed as a discipline in the 1940's, motivated initially by the need to solve complex planning problems in wartime operations. Its development accelerated rapidly in the postwar period as many industries found valuable uses for linear programming. The founders of the subject are generally regarded as George B. Dantzig, who devised the simplex method in 1947, and John von Neumann, who established the theory of duality that same year. The Nobel prize in economics was awarded in 1975 to the mathematician Leonid Kantorovich (USSR) and the economist Tjalling Koopmans (USA) for their contributions to the theory of optimal allocation of resources, in which linear programming played a key role. Many industries use linear programming as a standard tool, e.g. to allocate a finite set of resources in an optimal way. Examples of important application areas include airline crew scheduling, shipping or telecommunication networks, oil refining and blending, and stock and bond portfolio selection.

Linear programming (LP) is one of the most important general methods of operations research. Countless optimization problems can be formulated and solved using LP techniques. Operations research (OR) is a discipline explicitly devoted to aiding decision makers.

Operations research was born with the increasing need to solve optimal resource allocation during WWII

• Air Battle of Britain

• North Atlantic supply routing problems

• Optimal allocation of military convoys in Europe

1.2 PRINCIPLES OF MATHEMATICAL PROGRAMMING

Mathematical programming is a general technique to solve resource allocation problems using optimization. Mathematical models are designed to have optimal (best) solutions. Optimization problems are real world problems we encounter in many areas such as mathematics, engineering, science, business and economics. In these problems, we find the optimal, or most efficient, way of using limited resources to achieve the objective of the situation. This may be maximizing the profit, minimizing the cost, minimizing the total distance travelled or minimizing the total time to complete a project. For the given problem

1

we formulate a mathematical description called a mathematical model to represent the situation. Types of problems:

• Linear programming

• Integer programming

• Dynamic programming

• Decision analysis

• Network analysis and CPM (Critical Path Method)

1.3 LINEAR PROGRAMMING

Company managers are often faced with decisions relating to the use of limited resources. These resources may include men, materials and money. In other sector, there are insufficient resources available to do as many things as management would wish. The problem is based on how to decide on which resources would be allocated to obtain the best result, which may relate to profit or cost or both. Linear Programming is heavily used in Micro-Economics and Company Management such as Planning, Production, Transportation, Technology and other issues. Although the modern management issues are ever changing, most companies would like to maximize profits or minimize cost with limited resources. Therefore, many issues can be characterized as Linear Programming Problems (Sivarethinamohan, 2008). A linear programming model can be formulated and solutions derived to determine the best course of action within the constraint that exists. The model consists of the objective function and certain constraints.

 A typical mathematical program consists of a single objective function, representing either a profit to be maximized or a cost to be minimized, and a set of constraints that circumscribe the decision variables. In the case of a linear program (LP) the objective function and constraints are all linear functions of the decision variables. At first glance these restrictions would seem to limit the scope of the LP model, but this is hardly the case. Because of its simplicity, software has been developed that is capable of solving problems containing millions of variables and tens of thousands of constraints. Countless real-world applications have been successfully modeled and solved using linear programming techniques.

It is defined as a specific class of mathematical problem, in which a linear objective function is maximized (or minimized) subject to given linear constraints. This problem class is broad enough to encompass many interesting and important applications, yet specific enough to be tractable even if the number of variables is large.

Typical optimization problems maximize or minimize the value of a given variable (such as profit, total costs, etc.) when other specified variables (production capacity, required product quantities, etc.) are constrained. The field of mathematical programming includes a number of optimization methods, each described by a mathematical model. In such a model, there is one expression– the objective function – that should be maximized or minimized (or in some cases set to a desired value). In addition, the model must include constraints that are described by mathematical expressions. The most widely used models include only linear relationships, and belong to the field of linear programming. In such models both the objective function and the constraints are linear mathematical expressions. Mathematical model is a set of equations and inequalities that describe a system.

1.3.1 Limitations of Linear Programming Model

- It is applicable to only static situations since it does not take into account the effect of time. The OR team must define the objective function and constraints which can change due to internal as well as external forces.

- It assumes that the values of the coefficients of decision variables in the objective function as well in all the constraints are known with certainity. Since in most of the business situations, the decision variable coefficients are known only probabilistically, it cannot be applied to such situations.

- In some situations it is not possible to express both the objective function and constraints in linear form. For example, in production planning we often have non-linear constraints on production capacities like setup and takedown times which are often independent of the quantities produced. The misapplication of LP under non-linear conditions usually result in an incorrect solution.

- Linear programming deals with problems that have a single objective. Real life problems may involve multiple and even conflicting objectives. One has to apply goal programming under such situations.

When comparison is made between the advantages and disadvantages/limitations of LP, its advantages clearly overweigh its limitations. It must be clearly understood that LP techniques, like other mathematical tools only help the manager to take better decisions; they are in no way a substitute for the manager.

1.4 MOTIVATION

When we refer to resources we are talking about all the things that are required for production and operations. Included in this term are personnel, machines and equipment, cash, capital funds, material and supplies, utilities, floor space, time and other resources. These are the means of production and one or more may be scarce to each operations manager's particular situation. *The dominant question for the users of these resources is : Can we get the quantities of what we need when we need them ?*Many companies have had great success in recent years using operations research(OR) tools such as linear programming ,simulation, and decision analysis to reduce costs and improve their operations. One of the best ways to determine how best to allocate the scarce resources is with the use of Linear Programming (LP). Five common types of LP problems encountered are: product mix, ingredient mix, transportation, production plan, and assignment. Depending upon each problem type which could be described by posing three questions about each problem:

Q1.What is the single management objective?

Q2. What information do we need to achieve our objective?

Q3. What factors restrain us from achieving our objective?

The problem types as listed above are directly or indirectly of strategic importance to POM. Such real-world decisions often involve hundreds or even thousands of constraints, large quantities of data, many products and services, many time periods, numerous decision alternatives and other complications. The complexity of these constrained decisions prompted the development of linear programming methods. LP is a powerful tool in POM-powerful because of the variety of uses to which it is put by operations managers. The ability to think in terms of optimizing an objective within a set of constraints in real POM decision situations will definitely set a manager apart. This thinking is at the heart of linear programming.

1.4.1 Examples of successful LP application

- Scheduling school buses to minimize total distance traveled.

- Allocating police patrols to high crime areas to minimize response time.

- Scheduling tellers at banks to minimize total cost of labor.

- Blending raw materials in feed mills to maximize profit while producing animal feed.

- Selecting the product mix in a factory to make best use of available machine-hours and labor-hours available while maximizing profit.

4

- Allocating space for tenants in a shopping mall to maximize revenues to the leasing company.

- Crew scheduling problems

- Network flow models

- Pollution control and removal

- Estimation techniques

1.5 CHARACTERISTICS OF LINEAR PROGRAMMING

a) Deterministic (no probabilities).
b) Single Objective: *maximize* or *minimize* some quantity (the objective function).
c) Continuous decision variables (unknowns to be determined)
d) Constraints limit ability to achieve objectives.
e) Objectives and constraints must be expressed as *linear* equations or inequalities

The concept behind a linear programming problem is simple. It consists of the following terminology:

Decision Variables	Decision variables describe the quantities that the decision makers would like to determine. They are the unknowns of a mathematical programming model. Typically we will determine their optimum values with an optimization method. In a general model, decision variables are given algebraic designations such as $x_1, x_2, x_3 \ldots x_n$. The number of decision variables is n, and x_j is the name of the jth variable. In a specific situation, it is often convenient to use other names such as x_{ij} or y_i or $z(i, j)$. In computer models we use names such as FLOW1 or AB_5 to represent specific problem-related quantities. An assignment of values to all variables in a problem is called a solution.
Objective Function	The objective function evaluates some quantitative criterion of immediate importance such as cost, profit, utility, or yield. The general linear objective

5

function can be written as

$$z = c_1 x_1 + c_2 x_2 + \ldots + c_n x_n = \sum_{j=1}^{n} c_j x_j$$

Here c_j is the coefficient of the jth decision variable. The criterion selected can be either maximized or minimized.

| **Constraints** | A constraint is an inequality or equality defining limitations on decisions. Constraints arise from a variety of sources such as limited resources, contractual obligations, or physical laws. In general, an LP is said to have m linear constraints that can be stated as |

$$\sum_{j=1}^{n} a_{ij} x_j \begin{Bmatrix} \leq \\ = \\ \geq \end{Bmatrix} b_i, \text{ for } i = 1 \ldots m$$

One of the three relations shown in the large brackets must be chosen for each constraint. The number a_{ij} is called a "technological coefficient," and the number b_i is called the "right-hand side" value of the ith constraint. Strict inequalities ($<$ and $>$) are not permitted. When formulating a model, it is good practice to give a name to each constraint that reflects its purpose.

| **Simple Upper Bound** | Associated with each variable, x_j, may be a specified quantity, u_j, that limits its value from above; |

$$x_j \leq u_j, \text{for } j = 1 \ldots n$$

When a simple upper is not specified for a variable, the variable is said to be unbounded from above.

| **Nonnegativity Restrictions** | In most practical problems the variables are required to be nonnegative; |

$$x_j \geq 0, \text{for } j = 1 \ldots n$$

This special kind of constraint is called a non-negativity restriction. Sometimes variables are required to be non-positive or, in fact, may be unrestricted   (allowing   any   real   value).

Complete Linear Programming Model	Combining the aforementioned components into a single statement gives:

$$\text{Maximize or Minimize } z = \sum_{j=1}^{n} c_j x_j$$

subject to

$$\sum_{j=1}^{n} a_{ij} x_j \begin{Bmatrix} \leq \\ = \\ \geq \end{Bmatrix} b_i, \text{ for } i = 1 \ldots m$$

$$0 \leq x_j \leq u_j \text{ for } j = 1 \ldots n$$

The constraints, including non-negativity and simple upper bounds, define the feasible region of a problem. If minimization is desired instead of maximization, this can be accomplished by reversing the signs of $c_1 \ldots c_n$.

Parameters	The collection of coefficients (c_j, a_{ij}, b_i, u_j) for all values of the indices i and j are called the parameters of the model. For the model to be completely determined all parameter values must be known.

1.6 SOLVING LP PROBLEMS

In 1947 George Dantzig developed the simplex method of LP. Dantzig's simplex method was probably the beginning of the development of the present – day field of mathematical programming. The graphical solution approach conceptually demonstrates the process of LP solutions to those who have no experience with LP. Graphical solutions are therefore intended as a teaching tool to assist you in understanding the process of LP solutions. The simplex, transportation, and assignment methods are the practical LP solution tools. Although use of the simplex method by hand to solve LPs is tedious and error prone, enough standard LP computer programs are available for this task that real LP problems are always solved on computers . Several computer programs are available to solve LP problems:

•LINDO - Linear INteractive Discrete Optimizer   •GAMS - also solves non linear problems
•Matlab Toolbox - Optimization toolbox (from Mathworks)
•Excel Solver

1.7 BASIC STEPS FOR SOLVING A LINEAR PROGRAMMING MODEL

i) Recognize the problem
ii) Define the problem

iii) Define the decision variables

iv) Collect the necessary parametric data

v) Formulate a model

vi) Solve the model.

vii) Verify and validate the model

viii) Analyze model output

ix) Interpret model results

x) Recommend a course of action.

1.7.1 Recognize the problem

Before a problem can be analyzed, one must become aware of the existence of a **problem**. In the real world, problems hardly ever come pre-identified as such. One must proactively search for and identify problems. This must be done carefully because the apparent problem one perceives may not be the real problem. The analyst must distinguish between symptoms and actual problems. **Symptoms** are signs that indicate the existence of certain conditions, typically anomalous, somewhere in the system. A symptom is a reflection of some root cause. Treating a symptom, doctors well know, will not cure the underlying illness. The analyst must strive to uncover root causes and not be misled by superficial appearances.

Another important point is the type of problem present. The word *problem* has a negative or pejorative connotation: something is not going right. Let us call these **negative problems**. A negative problem exists when actual system performance falls below standards or expectations, creating a **performance gap**. The greater the performance gap, the greater the problem. Negative problems must be corrected promptly, for underperforming systems in competitive Darwinian environments such as the business world will inexorably be driven into extinction. In passing, keep in mind that there are two basic ways for performance gaps to arise: (1) the system may be under performing or (2) the performance standards/expectations may be set at unrealistically high levels. If the latter is the case, then the standards/expectations must be revised so as to make them attainable. Unattainable system states are immediately excluded from consideration in all system-analytic methods, including LP, for there is nothing to be done about things which are impossible.

More important, however, are the **positive problems**: novel opportunities that perhaps should be pursued. Negative problems must be corrected so that attention can be focused on finding positive problems and capitalizing on the opportunity they present *before our competitors do so*. Positive problems represent the future, and may well prove to be more profitable in the long run than continuing with present activities. Positive problems are generally harder to

8

detect, for no symptoms may exist or be apparent. To detect opportunities, visionary leadership is essential. It takes visionaries to convert negative problems into novel opportunities. There is another useful way to classify problems: urgency vs. importance. **Urgent problems** are those that demand immediate attention, although the solution need not be optimal.

Negative problems are often of this type. **Important problems**, on the other hand, require thorough attention and usually call for well-planned or optimal solutions. Urgent problems can typically be treated with a quick but effective solution, which may be temporary, whereas important problems entail considerable effort to devise efficient long-term solutions. Of course, a problem can be both urgent and important; therefore, be analytically prepared.

1.7.2 Define the problem

Linear programming requires that the analyst clearly define two fundamental aspects of the problem:

Objective: the system state or performance level one aims to attain

Constraints: the requirements that must be met by the proposed solution

Specifying the objective and all relevant constraints constitutes a complete LP problem definition.

1.7.3 Define the decision variables

A **decision variable** is a system setting whose value is assigned by the decision maker. A decision is made when a value is specified for a decision variable. Decision variables are sometimes called **controllable variables** because they are under the control of the decision maker. Decision variables are defined by specifying the metric (standard of measurement) used for quantification, the entity being referenced and the time span of reference. The time span may be omitted if the problem calls for a one-time or single-period decision.

Examples:

a) Let x = dozens of widgets produced per hour

b) Let y = pounds of chocolate consumed per person per week

c) Let z_i = dollars invested in financial instrument i (i = 1, 2, ..., n)

1.7.4 Collect the necessary parametric data

Many, if not most of the elements needed to model the system of interest are not under the control of the decision maker. For instance, in manufacturing systems, products must comply with detailed specifications, production processes follow fixed operating procedures, and financial aspects are strictly budgeted. These requirements are normally quantified by the people involved in those activities, such as engineering and accounting & finance. The

9

analyst must collect this information. Any piece of information in the form of a constant quantity is called a parameter. A **parameter** is simply a numerical constant that specifies particular system attributes. Sometimes system requirements vary depending on certain other factors, in which case they are known as **uncontrollable variables**.

1.7.5 Formulate a model

In LP, model formulation means expressing the objective and each of the constraints algebraically in terms of the decision variables and parameters. This is usually straightforward if the problem and the decision variables have been defined correctly. Difficulties in model formulation are typically a sign that something was amiss when defining the problem or the decision variables. Make sure steps 1 and 2 are complete and correct (coherent) before attempting to formulate a model.

There may be several possible ways to model the same problem. Which way is best depends on what information the analyst wants to obtain from the analysis. It is advisable to begin with a relatively simple model at the outset and subsequently refine it if additional information is desired.

1.7.6 Solve the model

Model solution in LP is computationally intensive and normally conducted by means of computer software. In this module, we will examine the graphical solution method to illustrate the basic concepts of LP. But the graphical method, although theoretically sound, is very limited in power and therefore practically useless for real-world applications. We will make use of MATLAB and Excel's Solver Add-In to illustrate a practical solution method. There are many software options available, however, all of which provide the same basic information regarding LP solutions.

1.7.7 Verify and validate the model

Model verification means ensuring that the model is computationally correct, that it calculates what it is supposed to. A model containing errors (of both omission and commission) is useless. **Model validation** means ensuring that the model is representationally correct, that it accurately reproduces the behavior of the real-world system being modeled. Verification deals with the internal consistency of the model while validation addresses its external (representational) correctness. In LP, verifying and validating a model can range from a simple inspection of the output to detailed comparisons of model results to the system's operational statistics.

1.7.8 Analyze model output

The computer provides the solution to the LP problem along with a sensitivity analysis. However, in LP the term **solution** means the optimal quantities the model assigns to the decision variables. The term **value** means the result obtained for the objective function with that **optimal solution**. The term **optimal** means the best possible value that complies with all problem constraints, one that maximizes or minimizes the value of the objective function. **Sensitivity analysis** consists of additional information provided by the model. This includes the **opportunity costs** (called **shadow prices** or **dual prices**) for all resources, the ranges in which these dual prices hold, and the range where the model solution remains valid if the objective function parameters (called objective function coefficients) were to change. Keep in mind that a model is an idealized representation of a real-world system and therefore the model solution is also an idealized result. In order to make effective use of model results, the next step must be performed.

1.7.9 Interpret model results

Every model is a simplification of the actual system being analyzed. Thus model solutions must be interpreted in the light of real-world considerations that may deviate from the simplifying assumptions built into the model. One way of dealing with this is to work interactively with the model to assess the impact of different possible conditions on model results. A great deal can be learned about system behavior by experimenting with the model, without affecting the actual system. The insight thus gained can be extremely useful for managers in the implementation phase of the project as well as in control of operations.

1.7.10 Recommend a course of action

Presentation of the findings concludes the LP modeling analysis includes sensitivity analysis, parametric analysis and sequence modeling.

1.8 FORMULATING LP PROBLEMS

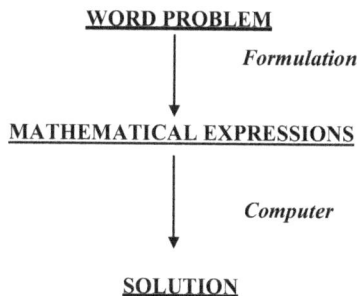

<u>**WORD PROBLEM**</u>

Formulation

<u>**MATHEMATICAL EXPRESSIONS**</u>

Computer

<u>**SOLUTION**</u>

Fig 1.1 Flow chart of formulation of LP problem

11

1.9 OBJECTIVES OF THE STUDY

The objectives of the study are listed below:

- Detailed study of how LP can be used to support strategic management decisions and objectives achieved within constraints imposed on organizations.
- Formulate a linear programming model for a given problem.
- Solve linear programming models using **MATLAB & Excel Solver** to find an optimal solution.
- Analyze the information provided in answer report, sensitivity analysis and parametric analysis to study the affect of discrete and continuous changes in model parameters on the optimal solution.
- To identify the bottle-necks.
- To determine the optimal sequence needed to process jobs on various machines and to calculate the total time needed to complete the jobs.
- To recommend a course of action.

1.10 ORGANISATION OF THE STUDY

This study is organized as follows. Chapter 1 provides the motivation and objectives of the dissertation. Chapter 2 provides a brief literature review relevant to the dissertation. Chapter 3 explains the problem statement and its optimal solution using MATLAB and Excel Solver. It provides the optimal scheduling to minimize the total processing time for two products using graphical method and Gantt chart. Chapter 4 provides Sensitivity Analysis using Excel Solver and Parametric Analysis using Jensen LP Solver. Chapter 5 summarizes the results and recommends a course of action. Chapter 6 concludes the dissertation and provides the scope for future work.

1.11 SUMMARY

The motivation and objectives of the present work and organization of the study were explained in this chapter. The subsequent chapter provides a review of relevant literature.

CHAPTER 2
LITERATURE REVIEW

2.1 INTRODUCTION

Today, perhaps more than ever before, operations managers understand that most decisions must be made and objectives achieved with in constraints imposed on organizations. Customer demand for products and services, limited production resources, government regulations, quality requirements, and technological limitations are examples of constraints in POM. Within these and other constraints, managers seek to accomplish their operation strategies. At world class companies, managers at all levels use the power of linear programming and other analysis tools to solve complex, constrained business problems. *LP is applied to both strategic, one-of-a-kind, long range decisions and short range, recurring decisions.* Both types can be of strategic importance in equipping a company for competition in a highly competitive industry.

A brief literature review of the topics that has been covered in this work is provided in this chapter. The review takes into account most of the relevant work that has been published and are accessible, on the topics under study. The journals, books and other resources used are mentioned below and documented in the reference section.

2.2 DECISION MAKING IN POM
Norman Gaither & Greg Frazier. Operations Management. Cengage Learning,2009

According to authors no other approach helps us understand how operations managers manage than the examination of the decisions in POM, because in large part ,operations managers manage decisions about all the activities of production systems.

Of the many functions in business there are three primary functions: operations, marketing, and finance/accounting.POM is nothing but Production and Operations management responsible for the management of an organization's productive resources or its production system, which converts inputs into the organization's products and services. This conversion process is the heart of what is called operations or production. Without operations, no products or services could be produced; without marketing, no products or services could be sold ;without finance/accounting, financial failure would surely result. Achievement of the organizational goals of profitability, survival, and growth dynamic business climate requires cooperative teamwork among these primary business functions. In this study, we shall pay particular attention to the decisions that operations managers make and how they make them.

Classifying operations decisions is difficult, but in our experience as operations managers, decisions tended to fall into three general categories:

Strategic decisions : Decisions about products, processes, and facilities. These decisions are of strategic importance and have long-term significance for the organization. It concern operations strategies and the long-range game plan for the firm. These decisions are so important that typically people from production or operations, personnel, engineering, marketing, and finance get together to study the business opportunities carefully and to arrive at a decision that puts the organization in the best position for achieving its long-term goals. Examples of this type of planning decision are:

- Deciding whether to launch a new –product development project
- Deciding on the design for a production process for a new product
- Deciding how to allocate scarce materials, utilities, capacity ,and personnel among new and existing business opportunities
- Deciding what new facilities are needed and where to locate them

Operating decisions :Decisions about planning production to meet demand. These decisions are necessary if the ongoing production of goods and services is to satisfy the demands of the market and provide profits for the company. The principal responsibility of operations is to take the orders for products and services from customers, which the marketing function has generated, and deliver products and services in such a way that there are satisfied customers at reasonable costs. In carryout this responsibility, numerous decisions are made. Examples of this type of decision are:

- Deciding how much finished-goods inventory to carry out for each product.
- Deciding what products and how much of each to include in next month's production schedule.
- Deciding how many temporary employees to hire next week.
- Deciding how much to purchase from each vendor next month. Such decisions are fundamental to the success of the production function and the entire organization.

Control decisions : Decisions about planning and controlling operations. These decisions concern day to day activities of workers, quality of products and services, production and overhead costs. And maintenance of equipment. Examples of this type of decision are

- Deciding what to do about a department's failure to meet the planned labor cost target.
- Developing labor cost standards for a revised product design that is about to go into production.
- Deciding what the new quality control acceptance criteria should be for a product that has had a change in design.
- Deciding how often to perform preventive maintenance on a key piece of equipment.

Operations management is the management of an organization's productive resources or its productive system, which converts inputs into the organization's products and services.

On the other hand Operations Research approaches problem solving and decision making from the total's system perspective.

2.3 THE SIMPLEX METHOD.

Michael L. Overton, Linear Programming, Draft for Encyclopedia Americana, December 20,1997

The simplex method has been the standard technique for solving a linear program since the 1940's. In brief, the simplex method passes from vertex to vertex on the boundary of the feasible polyhedron, repeatedly increasing the objective function until either an optimal solution is found, or it is established that no solution exists. In principle, the time required might be an exponential function of the number of variables, and this can happen in some contrived cases. In practice, however, the method is highly efficient, typically requiring a number of steps which is just a small multiple of the number of variables. Linear programs in thousands or even millions of variables are routinely solved using the simplex method on modern computers. Efficient, highly sophisticated implementations are available in the form of computer software packages.

2.4 THE COMMAND *linprog*

Jan Verschelde, UIC, Dept of Math, Stat & CS MATLAB Lecture 9, page 2, Apr 2008

The command linprog from the optimization toolbox implements the simplex algorithm to solve a linear programming problem in the form:

$$\min_{x} f * x$$

subject to A * x ≤ b

where f is any vector and the matrix A and vector b define the linear constraints.

The optimization toolbox has the command *linprog*:

>> *linprog*(f,A,b) % optimize

>> -f*ans % compute profit

The latest versions of MATLAB have the command *simlp,* which is very much like *linprog.*

2.5 USING EXCEL SOLVER IN OPTIMIZATION PROBLEMS

Leslie Chandrakantha ,John Jay College of Criminal Justice of CUNY ,Mathematics and Computer Science Department ,445 West 59th Street, New York, NY 10019

The author illustrates the use of spreadsheet modeling and Excel Solver in solving linear and nonlinear programming problems in an introductory Operations Research course. This is especially useful for interdisciplinary courses involving optimization problems. They work through examples from different areas such as manufacturing, transportation, financial planning, and scheduling to demonstrate the use of Solver.

In this paper they have shown how to use spreadsheet modeling and Excel Solver for solving linear and nonlinear programming problems. Optimization problems are real world problems we encounter in many areas such as mathematics, engineering, science, business and economics. In these problems, we find the optimal, or most efficient, way of using limited resources to achieve the objective of the situation. This may be maximizing the profit, minimizing the cost, minimizing the total distance travelled or minimizing the total time to complete a project. For the given problem, we formulate a mathematical description called a mathematical model to represent the situation. The model consists of following components:

• Decision variables: The decisions of the problem are represented using symbols such as X1, X2, X3,…..Xn. These variables represent unknown quantities (number of items to produce, amounts of money to invest in and so on).

• Objective function: The objective of the problem is expressed as a mathematical expression in decision variables. The objective may be maximizing the profit, minimizing the cost, distance, time, etc.,

• Constraints: The limitations or requirements of the problem are expressed as inequalities or equations in decision variables. If the model consists of a linear objective function and linear constraints in decision variables, it is called a linear programming model. A nonlinear programming model consists of a nonlinear objective function and nonlinear constraints. Linear programming is a technique used to solve models with linear objective

16

function and linear constraints. The Simplex Algorithm developed by Dantzig (1963) is used to solve linear programming problems. This technique can be used to solve problems in two or higher dimensions..

2.5.1 Spreadsheet Modeling and Excel Solver

A mathematical model implemented in a spreadsheet is called a spreadsheet model. Major spreadsheet packages come with a built-in optimization tool called Solver. Now we demonstrate how to use Excel spreadsheet modeling and Solver to find the optimal solution of optimization problems. If the model has two variables, the graphical method can be used to solve the model. Very few real world problems involve only two variables. For problems with more than two variables, we need to use complex techniques and tedious calculations to find the optimal solution. The spreadsheet and solver approach makes solving optimization problems a fairly simple task and it is more useful for students who do not have strong mathematics background. The first step is to organize the spreadsheet to represent the model. We use separate cells to represent decision variables, create a formula in a cell to represent the objective function and create a formula in a cell for each constraint left hand side. Once the model is implemented in a spreadsheet, next step is to use the Solver to find the solution. In the Solver, we need to identify the locations (cells) of objective function, decision variables, nature of the objective function (maximize/minimize)and constraint.

2.6 PRODUCTION OUTSOURCING: A LINEAR PROGRAMMING MODEL FOR THE THEORY OF CONSTRAINTS

Alex Coman and Boaz Ronen, International Journal of Production Research, 2000, vol. 38, no. 7, 1631-1639

This paper presents an analysis of the outsourcing problem. Pertinent variables are identified and the relationships between them are defined. They formulated the outsourcing problem as a LP problem and identified an analytical solution. An example having three decision models : standard cost accounting, standard Theory-Of-Constraints (TOC) and our own solution. The model enables managers to determine which products to manufacture and which to outsource. The solution of the LP formulation enables the managers to apply the model by computing an operational ratio, without having to solve a LP problem. The final model is simpler to apply and requires the computation of fewer variables than other prevalent models.

2.7 GENERAL RESOURCE ALLOCATION MODEL

Operations Research Models and Methods, by Paul A. Jensen and Jonathan F. Bard, published by John Wiley and Sons in 2003

Linear programming is a widely used model type that can solve decision problems with many thousands of variables. Generally, the feasible values of the decisions are delimited by a set of constraints that are described by mathematical functions of the decision variables. The feasible decisions are compared using an objective function that depends on the decision variables. For a linear program the objective function and constraints are required to be linearly related to the variables of the problem. It is common to describe a problem class with a general algebraic model where numeric values are represented by lower case letters usually drawn from the early part of the alphabet. Variables are given alphabetical representations generally drawn from the later in the alphabet. Terms are combined with summation signs. The general resource allocation model is below. When the parameters are given specific numerical values the result is an *nstance* of he general model.

Parameters

n = Number of activities. Activities are indexed by $j = 1 \ldots n$

m = Number of resources. Resources are indexed by $i = 1 \ldots m$

P_j = Profit for activity j

b_i = Amount available of resource i

a_{ij} = Amount of resource i used by a unit of activity j.

Variables

x_j = Amount of activity j selected

Model

Maximize or Minimize $z = \sum_{j=1}^{n} c_j x_j$

subject to

$$\sum_{j=1}^{n} a_{ij} x_j \begin{Bmatrix} \leq \\ = \\ \geq \end{Bmatrix} b_i, \text{ for } i = 1 \ldots m$$

$0 \leq x_j \leq u_j$ for $j = 1 \ldots n$

2.8. SUMMARY

A brief summary of literature relevant to this study was provided in this chapter. The subsequent chapter provides the details about developing a valid linear programming model which is a typical product-mix type problem in a manufacturing system.

CHAPTER 3
LINEAR PROGRAMMING MODEL

3.1 INTRODUCTION

Most operations research studies involve the construction of a mathematical model. The model is a collection of logical and mathematical relationships that represents aspects of the situation under study. Models describe important relationships between variables, include an objective function with which alternative solutions are evaluated, and constraints that restrict solutions to feasible values. What are the characteristics of problems suitable for LP solutions? Table 3.1 outlines briefly the four basic problems characteristics .When all of these requirements are met. LP can be a suitable tool of analysis.

A well-defined single objective must be stated.
There must be alternative courses of action.
The total achievement of the objective must be constrained by scarce resources or other resources.
The objective and each of the constraints must be expressed as linear mathematical functions.

Table 3.1 Characteristics of LP Problems in POM.

Linear programming is a widely used model type that can solve decision problems with many thousands of variables. Generally, the feasible values of the decisions are delimited by a set of constraints that are described by mathematical functions of the decision variables. The feasible decisions are compared using an objective function that depends on the decision variables. For a linear program the objective function and constraints are required to be linearly related to the variables of the problem. The resource allocation problem, *a product-mix type* considered in this chapter illustrate that linear programming can be used in a practical situation with in the manufacturing system. We illustrate how a situation can be translated into a mathematical model, and how the model can be solved to find the optimum solution. The problem has been numerically solved using the MATLAB & Excel add-ins.

3.2 THE PROBLEM STATEMENT

One of the most widespread commercial applications of scientific computation is linear programming. It is widely used for allocating resources to achieve an objective. In my present work a product-mix problem is being illustrated and solved using MATLAB for its optimal solution. The optimal sequencing to process two products on four machines will be been carried out using graphical method and total minimum elapsed time (process time plus idle time) to manufacture both products will be found out using Gantt chart. The sensitivity analysis will be done to study the effect on optimal solution due to discrete change in parameters of LP problem with the help of Excel Solver. The parametric analysis will be done to study the effect on optimal solution due to continuous change in parameters of LP problem using computer software. Apart from these we have examined other options like product outsourcing, one-time cost, cross training of one operator and manufacturing of hypothetical third product on under-utilized machines.

The figure 3.1 represents a manufacturing system producing two products labeled P and Q. The rounded rectangles at the top of the figure indicate the revenue per unit and the maximum sales per week.

For instance we can sell as many as 100 units per week of P for $90 per unit. The circles show the raw materials used, and the rectangles indicate the operations that the products must pass through in the manufacturing process. Each rectangle designates a machine used for the operation and the time required. For example product P consists of two subassemblies. RM stands for raw material .To manufacture the first subassembly, one unit of RM1 passes through machine A for 15 minutes. The output of machine A is moved to machine C where it is processed for 10 minutes. The second subassembly starts with RM2 processed in machine B for 15 minutes. The output is taken to machine C for 5 minutes of processing. The two subassemblies are joined with a purchased part in machine D. The result is a finished unit of P. Product Q is manufactured by a similar process as indicated in the figure 3.1.

The rectangle at the upper left indicates that one machine of each type is available. Each machine operates for 2400 minutes per week. OE stands for operating expenses. For this case the operating expenses, not including the raw material cost is $6000. This amount is expended regardless of amounts of P and Q produced.

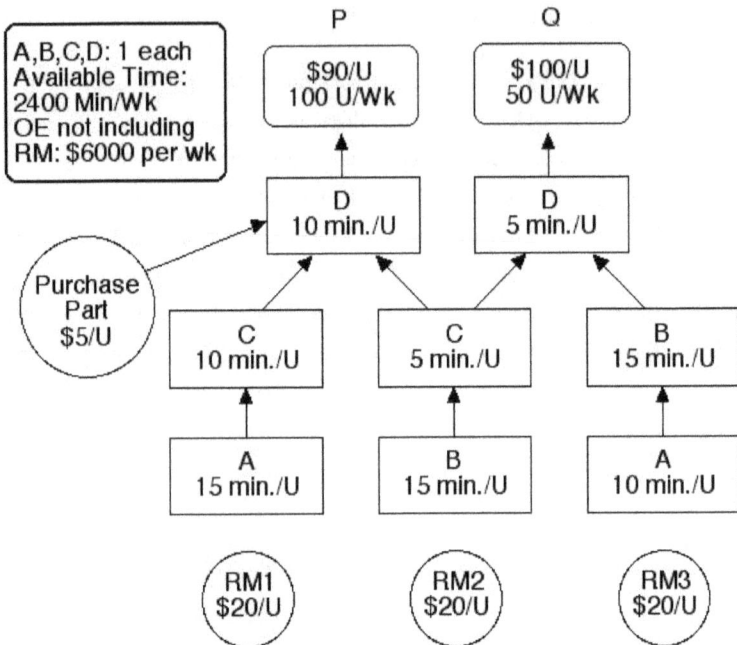

Fig 3.1 The resource time per product in minutes

. Our problems include the following:

i)   Find the product mix that maximizes profit. Identify the bottlenecks.
ii)   For each product, find the range over which the unit profit can change without affecting the product mix.
iii) For each machine, identify the marginal benefit of adding one more minute of machine time.
iv)   For each machine, find the range over which the time availability can change without affecting the identity of the bottleneck.
v)   To study Parametric Analysis of resource availability and resource consumed on machine B.
vi)   To determine the optimal order or sequence of processing two jobs through four machines that are arranged in a specific order so as to optimize the total time or cost.
vii) To recommend a course of action.

3.3 FORMULATION OF LP MODEL

There are many problems that might be posed regarding the PQ situation, but we choose the problem of allocating the times available on the machines to the manufacture of the two products. The decisions involve the amounts of the two products.

P = The amount of product P to produce in one week.

Q = The amount of product Q to produce in one week

The objective is to maximize profit. From the figure we see that the profit per unit of product is its unit revenue less the raw material cost per unit. For P the unit profit is \$45 and for Q it is \$60. The objective, Z is a linear expression of the amounts produced.

Objective Function

$$Z = 45P + 60Q \qquad \text{-------- (3.1)}$$

Machine Time Constraints

$$\text{Machine A} : 15\,P + 10\,Q \le 2400$$

$$\text{Machine B} : 15\,P + 30\,Q \le 2400$$

$$\text{Machine C} : 15\,P + 5\,Q \le 2400$$

$$\text{Machine D} : 10\,P + 5\,Q \le 2400 \quad \text{------ (3.2)}$$

Finally, we require that the amounts manufactured not exceed the demand determined by the markets for the products. We include the non-negativity requirement with the market constraints.

Market Constraints

$$P \le 100$$

$$Q \le 50 \qquad \text{------------------- (3.3)}$$

The linear model is complete. This simple case illustrates the required parts of the model. First we provide a word definition of each of the variables of the problem. Next we show the objective criterion with which alternatives are to be compared. Then we list the constraints that must be satisfied by a feasible solution. Each set of constraints should be named to describe the purpose of the constraint.

3.4 SOLUTION USING MATLAB

Since there are only two unknowns P and Q are involved indicated by x and y respectively, we may graph all constraints. The MATLAB commands given are as follows:

```
>> x=0:160                          % range of graph
>> y1=(2400-15.*x)./10;             % 15x+10y ≤ 2400 machine A
>> area(x,y1)
>> y2=max((2400-15.*x)./30,0);      % 15x+30y ≤ 2400 machine B
>> y3=max((2400-15.*x)./5,0);       % 15x+5y ≤ 2400 machine C
>> y4=max((2400-10.*x)/5,0);        % 10x+5y ≤ 2400 machine D
>> y5=max((100-1.*x)./0,0);         % 1x+0y ≤ 100    market P product
>> y6=max((50-0.*x)./1,0);          % 0x+1y ≤ 50     market Q product
>> ytop=min([y1;y2;y3;y4;y5;y6]);   % array of minima
>> area(x,ytop);                    % filled area plot
```

The shaded area enclosed by the constraints is called the feasible region, which is the set of points satisfying all the constraints. If this region is empty, then the problem is said to be infeasible, and it has no solution. The lines of equal profit Z are given by Z = 45x + 60y. If we fix Z to, say 100, then all points (x; y) which satisfy 45x + 60y yield the same profit 100.

```
>> hold on; [u v]= meshgrid(0:160,0:160);
>> contour(u,v,45*u+60*v);
>> hold off;
```

To find the optimal solution, we look at the lines of equal profit to find the corner of the feasible region which yields the highest profit. This corner can be found at the farthest line of equal profit which still touches the feasible region as shown in Fig 3.2

24

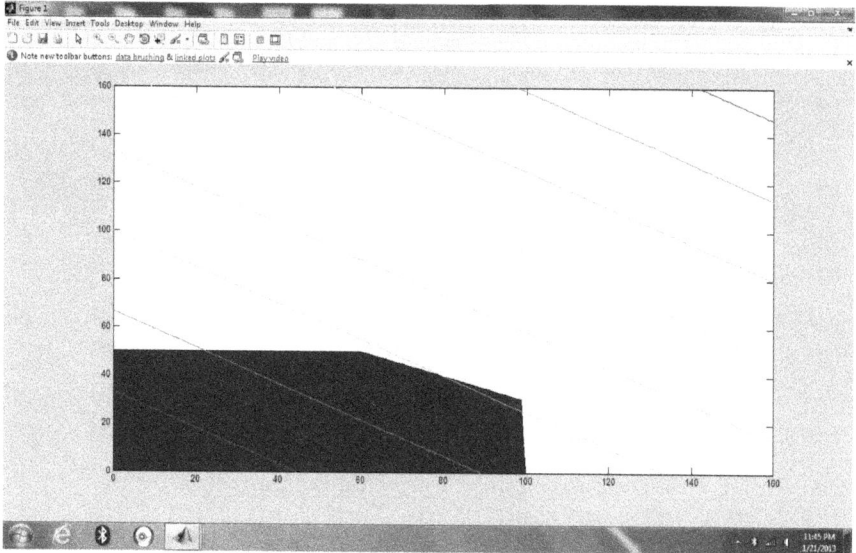

Fig 3.2 MATLAB graph

3.5 THE COMMAND *simlp*

The command *simlp* from the optimization toolbox implements the simplex algorithm to solve a linear programming problem in the form:

$$\min_{x} f * x$$

subject to $A * x \leq b$

where f is any vector and the matrix A and vector b define the linear constraints. So our original problem is translated into the format

$$\max_{x,y} \ 45x + 60y$$
subject to

$$\min_{x,y} \ -45x - 60y$$
subject to

$15x + 10y \leq 2400$	15	10		2400
$15x + 30y \leq 2400$	15	30		2400
$15x + 5y \leq 2400$	15	5	$\begin{bmatrix} -x^- \\ y \end{bmatrix}$	2400
$10x + 5y \leq 2400$	10	5	$\leq$	2400
$x \leq 100$	1	0		100
$y \leq 50$	0	1		50
$x \geq 0$	-1	0		0
$y \geq 0$	0	-1		0

Observe the switching of signs to turn the max into a min and to deal with the $\leq$ constraints.

25

Duality in linear programming is a very important concept, more than just a matter of formatting. The economical interpretation of duality can be simplified into the saying that minimizing the cost of production is equivalent to maximizing the profit.

Now we are ready to solve the problem. First we set up the vectors and matrices:

>> f=[-45 -60]

>> A=[15 10; 15 30;15 5; 10 5; 1 0; 0 1; -1 0; 0 -1]

>> b=[2400; 2400; 2400; 2400; 100; 50; 0; 0]

The optimization toolbox has the command *simlp* :

>> *simlp*(f,A,b)   % optimize

>> -f*ans   % compute profit

f =

  -45 -60

A =

  15 10
  15 30
  15   5
  10   5
   1   0
   0   1
  -1   0
   0 -1

b =

  2400
  2400
  2400
  2400
   100
    50
     0
     0

ans =

  100
   30

ans =

6300

3.6 THE OPTIMAL SOLUTION USING MATLAB

The final result as derived using MATLAB are as follows:

The values obtained are $X = 100$ units and $Y = 30$ units which mean that for the product mix to optimize profits the manufacturer should produce 100 units of P products per week and 30 units of Q products per week. The net profit would be equal to maximum revenue, Z minus total operating expenses, OE which comes out to be $300 per week

3.7 SOLUTION USING EXCEL SOLVER

The problem is to find values of P and Q that maximize the objective of the problem. We use the _Mathematical Programming_ add-in to generate the model in Excel. The model is then solved with the _Excel Solver_. The worksheet with the model is shown below.

	A	B	C	D	E	F	G	H
1								
2								
3	Decision variables	P	Q			Z	6300	
4	Values	100	30					
5	Objective cofficient	45	60					
6								
7								
8	Constraints			LHS	<,=,>	RHS		
9	Machine A	15	10	1800	≤	2400		
10	Machine B	15	30	2400	≤	2400		
11	Machine C	15	5	1650	≤	2400		
12	Machine D	10	5	1150	≤	2400		
13	Market P	1	0	100	≤	100		
14	Market Q	0	1	30	≤	50		
15								

Fig 3.3 Excel spreadsheet for a linear programming model

Figure 3.3 shows the initial spread sheet with following SUMPRODUCT formulas:

For Z value :

=B5*B4+C5*C4   (Initially the values for P and Q were taken as 0)

For LHS constraints:

Machine A : =B9*B$4+C9*C$4

27

Machine B : =B10*B$4+C10*C$4

Machine C : =B11*B$4+C11*C$4

Machine D := B12*B$4+C12*C$4

Figure 3.4 shows the solver Parameters window when Solver is selected from Excel Tools menu.(if Solver does not show as an option under the tools menu, then select Add-ins and check the box for Solver Add-in.) The cell address for _Set Target Cell' is where the objective function Z formula was entered. The cell, addresses for _By Changing Cells' are where the decision variables values were entered (initially entered as zeroes).To enter the constraints, click on Add button shown in Fig 3.4. The Add constraint window will then come up. For each constraint, the _Cell Reference' is where the LHS formula was entered and the _Constraint' is where the RHS value was entered in our spreadsheet. After all constraints are entered, click on the Options button

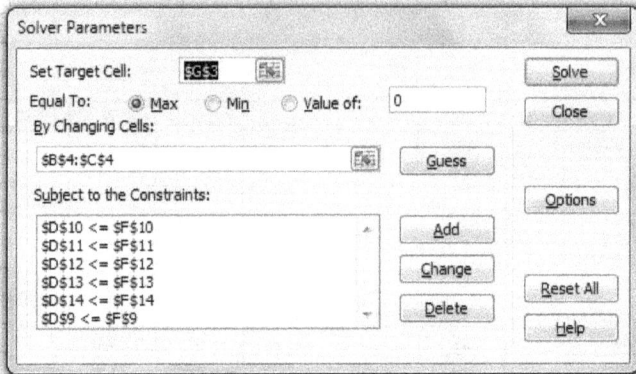

Fig 3.4 Solver Parameters dialogue box

shown in figure 3.4 and the Solver Options window will come up .The only options to change are checking the boxes for Assume Linear Model and Assume Non-Negative. After these have been checked, then click on the solver button shown figure 3.4.When Solver has found the solution, another window will come up; click on Answer Report and Sensitivity Report to generate these two reports. The optimal solution of the LP problem results in the return of the value 100 in cell B4 and of 30 in cell C5 (see Figure 3.3).The objective function value 6300 in cell G3. *This is consistent with the result from MATLAB.* The optimum solution is to produce 100 units of P and 30 units of Q. The net profit of this solution is $300. That is the

$6300 shown in cell G3 on the worksheet, less the $6000 operating expense. The latter was not included in the model because it does not affect the optimum decisions .Constant values are never included in the objective function.

3.8 OPTIMAL SCHEDULING ON MACHINES

The sequencing problem involves the determination of an optimal order or sequence of performing a series of jobs by a number of facilities (that are arranged in a specific order) so as to optimize the total time or cost. Such problems like our product-mix problem are encountered in _production shops' where different products are to be processed over various combinations of machines.

3.8.1 Assumptions in Sequencing problems

The following simplifying assumptions are usually made while dealing with sequencing problems :

    i)   Only one operation is carried out on a machine at a particular time.

    ii) Each operation, once started, must be completed.

    iii) An operation must be completed before its succeeding operation start.

    iv) Only one machine of each type is available.

    v)   A job is processed as soon as possible, but only in the order specified.

    vi) Processing times are independent of order of performing the operations.

    vii) The transportation time i.e, the time required to transport jobs from one machine to another machine is negligible.

    viii) Jobs are completely known and are ready for processing when the period under consideration starts.

    ix) The cost of in-process inventory for each job is same and negligibly small.

3.8.2 Processing Two Jobs through Four Machines

Let us consider the following situation of our product-mix problem :

    i)   There are 4 machines, denoted by A, B, C, and D

    ii) Only two products P and Q are to be manufactured.

    iii) The technological ordering of each of the two jobs through 4 machines is known. The ordering may or may not be the same for both jobs. Alternate ordering is not permissible for either job. In our case for product P it is B-A-C-D and for product

29

Q it is A-B-C-D.

iv) The actual or expected processing times are known as follows:

For product P as per ordering B-A-C-D, it is 15 min- 15 min- 15 min- 10 min respectively. For product Q as per ordering A-B-C-D, it is 10 min- 30 min- 5 min- 5 min respectively.

v) Each machine can work only one job at a time and storage space for in-process inventory is available.

The problem is to minimize the total elapsed time T i.e. to minimize the time from the start of first job to the completion of second job. Such a problem can be solved by graphical method which is simple and provides good (though not necessarily optimal) results. The graphical procedure is described with the help of following steps:

Step 1

Draw two axes at right angles to each other. Represent processing time on job P along horizontal axis and processing time on job Q along vertical axis. Scale used must be same for both the jobs.

Step 2

Layout the machine times for the two jobs on corresponding axes in the technological order. This is shown in figure 3.5.

Step 3

Machine B requires 15 minutes for job P and 30 minutes for job Q. A rectangle is thus constructed for machine B. Similar rectangles are constructed for machines A, C, and D as shown.

Step 4

Make a program by starting from origin O and moving through the various stages of completion (points) till the point marked _finish' is reached. Choose path consisting only of horizontal, vertical and 45° lines. A horizontal line represents work on job P while job Q remains idle; a vertical line represents work on job Q while job P remains idle and a 45° line to the base represents simultaneous work on both jobs.

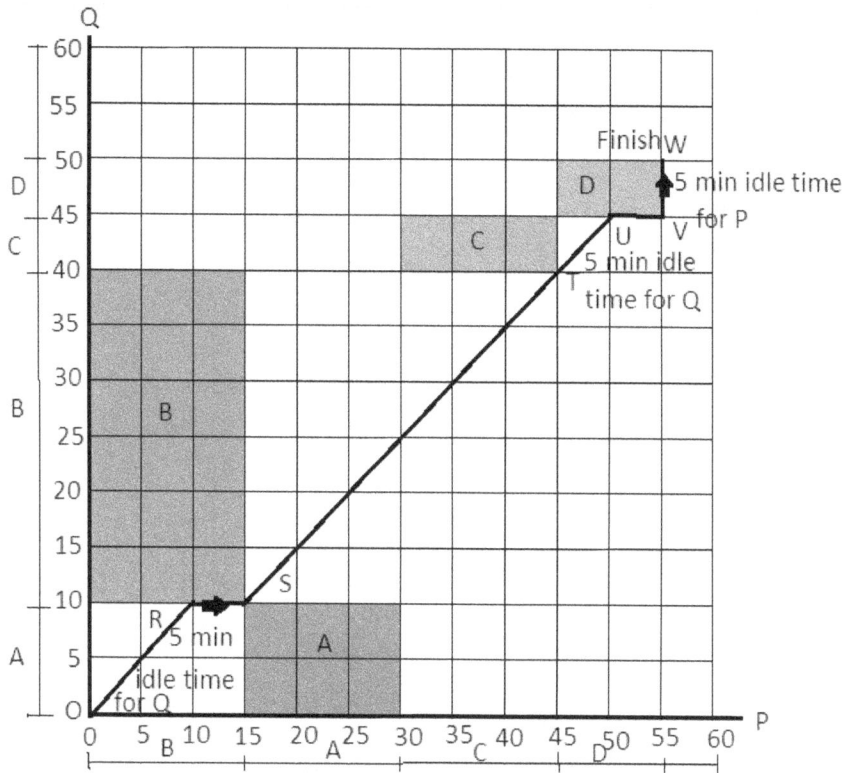

Fig 3.5 Graphical solution of 2 jobs and 4 machines

Step 5

Find the optimal path (program). An optimal path is one that minimizes idle time for job P (vertical movement). Likewise, an optimal path is one that minimizes idle time for job Q (horizontal movement). Obviously, the optimal path is one which coincides with 45° line to the maximum extent. Further, both jobs cannot be processed simultaneously on one machine.

Graphically, this means that diagonal movement through the blocked out areas is not allowed.

A good path, accordingly, is chosen by eye and drawn on the graph (path ORSTUVW).

Step 6

Find the elapsed time. It is obtained by adding the idle time for either job to the processing time for that job. The idle time for the chosen path is found to be 10 minutes for job Q and 5 minutes for job P.

Therefore, Total elapsed time = 55 + 5 = 60 minutes (considering job P)

= 50 + 10 = 60 minutes (considering job Q)

Step 7

The optimal schedule corresponding to the chosen path is shown in Gantt Chart as figure 3.6.

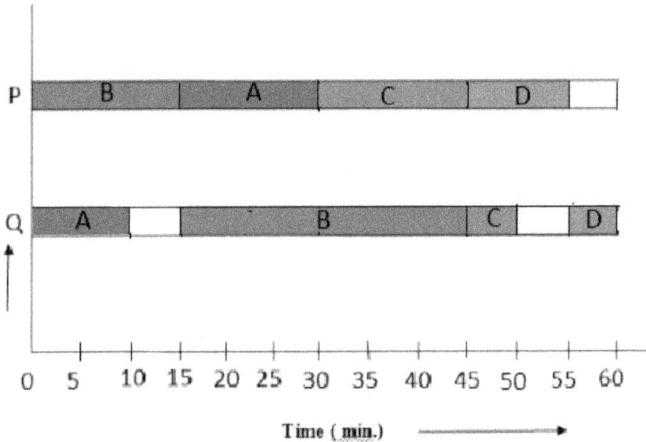

Fig 3.6 Gantt Chart

The optimal sequence or schedule on various machines for the two jobs as evident from Gantt Chart is:

Machine A : job Q precedes job P,

Machine B : job P precedes job Q,

Machine C : job P precedes job Q, and

32

Machine D : job P precedes job Q

3.9 SUMMARY

This is the most important chapter of thesis work because being able to recognize a product-mix problem for which LP solution is appropriate is fundamental. The characteristics of LP problem are clearly defined and formulated the problem in LP format. The optimal solutions are obtained using MATLAB and Excel Solver. The results derived are same in both cases. This proves that our LP model is valid for the given product-mix problem. Further analysis carried out on sequencing problem involving the determination of an optimal order or sequence of processing two jobs through four machines that are arranged in a specific order so as to optimize the total time or cost. The subsequent chapter explains how to interpret the meaning of the printouts of a solution of an LP problem from Excel Solver.

CHAPTER 4

INTERPRETING COMPUTER SOLUTIONS OF LP PROBLEM

4.1 INRODUCTION

In this chapter, we explain how to interpret the meaning of the printout of solution of an LP problem from Excel Solver. The reports generated by computer are indicative of the information that is commonly available when we solve a LP. We shall deal with each of them in turn. When Solver has found the optimum, the results dialog appears as shown in Fig 4.1 .Several optional reports may be selected.

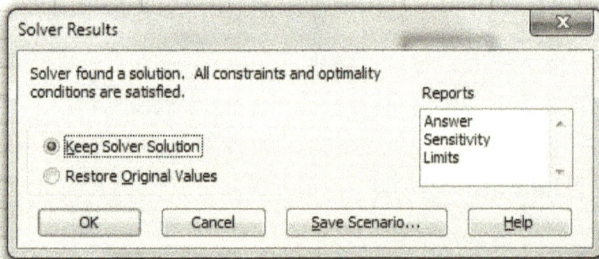

Fig 4.1 Solver Results dialogue box

The Answer report provides the optimal solution of LP problem and gives information about the slack. Sensitivity report provides reduced costs and sensitivity ranges for the variables, dual values and Sensitivity ranges for the constraint bounds. To interpret these reports one should be familiar with the following terms.

4.2 TERMS

Bottleneck — a limiting factor on the rate of an operation. A workstation operating at its maximum capacity becomes a bottleneck if the rate of production elsewhere in the plant increases but throughput at that workstation cannot be increased to meet demand.

Constraint — a restriction that must be observed (complied with)

Controllable variable — another name for decision variable.

Decision variable — a quantity that is under the control of and chosen by the decision maker (or determined by a decision model such as LP).

34

Dual price — a term somewhat synonymous with shadow price (there is a slight difference in how they are computed and interpreted, but they both represent the economic value of an additional unit of a resource.

Important problem — a situation of significance that calls for a carefully reasoned solution.

Model validation — ensuring that the model adequately represents the object system.

Model verification — ensuring that the model is computationally correct.

Negative problem — situation that exists when a system is underperforming.

Objective — the system state or performance level intended to be attained.

Objective function — an algebraic equation that states the end one seeks to achieve.

Opportunity cost — loss of potential gain from other alternatives incurred by choosing one course of action.

Optimal — the best possible alternative that satisfies a set of constraints.

Optimal solution — a solution that yields the best possible value (either maximum or minimum) for a given objective function and set of constraints.

Parameter — a numerical constant defining some system attribute.

Performance gap — the difference between actual system performance and established standards.

Positive problem — a situation or set of circumstances that offers advantageous prospects.

Problem — a matter, situation or state of affairs requiring a solution.

Reduced Cost

- The minimum amount by which the OFC of a variable should change to cause that variable to become non-zero.
- The amount by which the objective function value would change if the variable were forced to change from 0 to 1.

Sensitivity analysis — a procedure that determines the effect on the model solution and the value of the objective function for small changes in model parameters; a technique that throws light on the degree of stability of a given solution when the model is slightly altered.

Shadow price — the opportunity cost (economic value forgone) of not having one additional unit of a particular resource; the maximum premium one would be willing to pay for an additional unit of some resource.

Solution — a set of values for the decision variables that is feasible (complies with all constraints).

Symptom — a sign indicating the existence of some condition in a system.

Uncontrollable variable — a non-constant quantity that defines some system attribute.

Urgent problem — a situation demanding prompt attention.

Value — the numerical quantity generated by the objective function for a given solution.

4.2.1 Slack variables

A vertex of the feasible region can be defined by the corresponding values of the decision variables. These values can be determined algebraically.

Consider a set of LP constraints of the form

$$\Sigma_j \; A_{ij} \, x_j \; \le \; B_i \qquad\qquad (i = 1, 2, \ldots m; \; j = 1, 2, \ldots n)$$

This is equivalent to a set of simultaneous equations

$$\Sigma_j \; A_{ij} \, x_j + e_i = B_i$$

where the variables e_i are explicit *slack variables*.

4.2.2 Basic and non-basic variables

There are m equations and m + n unknowns (the decision variables and slacks) in this problem. A solution can be obtained by setting n variables to zero and finding the values of the remaining m variables. In a particular solution the variables which are set to zero are called non-basic variables and the variables for which values are calculated are called *basic variables*. The vertices of the feasible region are given by non-basic variables and basic variables. Note that setting a slack variable to zero is the same as stating that its constraint is one of the boundaries intersecting at the vertex. Such a constraint is described as *binding*. A solution which has been found by the above method is called a *basic solution*. If it satisfies all the LP constraints (i.e. all basic variables must be non-negative) it is called a *basic feasible solution*. This algebraic explanation can be extended to any general LP model. A solution produced by an LP code always includes a number of decision variables which are set equal to their upper or lower bounds, and constraints which are binding. These are called the *non-basic variables* and *non-basic* rows. The remaining variables and rows are described as basic. The total number of basic variables and rows in the solution is equal to m, the number of constraints. Note that the basic variables and rows are the only ones which can have values away from their limits. (This does not necessarily that the basic variables cannot have values equal to their limits). The set of basic variables and rows is called the *basis*.

4.3 ANSWER REPORT ANALYSIS

In this section we will study about the significance of slack variables as can be read from the answer report given in Fig 4.2. The Excel Solver solution showed that the optimal solution P=100 and Q=30 was given by the capacities of available resources Machine B and market demand of P product. These constraints are then said to be binding since their capacities /demand are fully utilized.

	A	B	C	D	E	F	G
1	Microsoft Excel 12.0 Answer Report						
2	Worksheet: [LPP1.xlsx]Sheet1						
3	Report Created: 4/29/2013 12:50:20 PM						
4							
5							
6	Target Cell (Max)						
7		Cell	Name	Original Value	Final Value		
8		$G$3	Z	0	6300		
9							
10							
11	Adjustable Cells						
12		Cell	Name	Original Value	Final Value		
13		$B$4	Values P	0	100		
14		$C$4	Values Q	0	30		
15							
16							
17	Constraints						
18		Cell	Name	Cell Value	Formula	Status	Slack
19		$D$9	Machine A LHS	1800	$D$9<=$F$9	Not Binding	600
20		$D$10	Machine B LHS	2400	$D$10<=$F$10	Binding	0
21		$D$11	Machine C LHS	1650	$D$11<=$F$11	Not Binding	750
22		$D$12	Machine D LHS	1150	$D$12<=$F$12	Not Binding	1250
23		$D$13	Market P LHS	100	$D$13<=$F$13	Binding	0
24		$D$14	Market Q LHS	30	$D$14<=$F$14	Not Binding	20
25							

Fig 4.2 Answer Report

The rest of the constraints are not binding, which means they have unused capacity. Capacity left over in the four resources can be calculated as the difference between available and used capacity. The unused capacity for a particular constraint is often referred to as its slack. The slack of the four constraints in our example can also be read from the answer report shown in Figure 4.2. The unused capacity in a constraint is often referred to as a slack variable.

4.4 SENSITIVITY ANALYSIS

Sensitivity analysis (see figure 4.3) is the study of how changes in model parameters affect the optimal solution. In Excel this information is provided in the sensitivity report. Let's take a closer look at some of the effects of various parameter changes.

	A	B	C	D	E	F	G	H
1	Microsoft Excel 12.0 Sensitivity Report							
2	Worksheet: [LPP1.xlsx]Sheet1							
3	Report Created: 4/29/2013 12:51:30 PM							
4								
5								
6	Adjustable Cells							
7				Final	Reduced	Objective	Allowable	Allowable
8		Cell	Name	Value	Cost	Coefficient	Increase	Decrease
9		$B$4	Values P	100	0	45	1E+30	15
10		$C$4	Values Q	30	0	60	30	60
11								
12	Constraints							
13				Final	Shadow	Constraint	Allowable	Allowable
14		Cell	Name	Value	Price	R.H. Side	Increase	Decrease
15		$D$9	Machine A LHS	1800	0	2400	1E+30	600
16		$D$10	Machine B LHS	2400	2	2400	600	900
17		$D$11	Machine C LHS	1650	0	2400	1E+30	750
18		$D$12	Machine D LHS	1150	0	2400	1E+30	1250
19		$D$13	Market P LHS	100	15	100	60	40
20		$D$14	Market Q LHS	30	0	50	1E+30	20
21								

Fig 4.3 Sensitivity Report

After arriving at the optimal solution to the product-mix problem that maximizes profit in chapter 3, we would now take the help of Sensitivity Report to solve the following remaining parts of our LP problem.

4.4.1 Find the Bottlenecks

From the value column for the constraints, we see the amounts of time required by the optimum production quantities. Clearly, the time on machine B is a bottleneck for this situation. The market for P is also a bottleneck because the optimum value is the upper bound for P. If either the time on machine B or the market for product P are increased, the profit will increase

4.4.2 Find the range over which the unit profit may change

This result is determined from the *sensitivity* analysis. We show below the sensitivity analysis created by the Excel Solver. The part of the analysis labeled *Adjustable Cells* provides information concerning the variables and the objective function. Each row on this table represents a variable. The *Cell* entry is the Excel reference to the cell holding the variable value for the optimum solution. The *Name* is provided by the name appearing above the value cell on the model worksheet. The *Final Value* is the amount of that variable for the optimum solution. The *Reduced Cost* is the minimum amount by which the OFC of a variable should change to cause that variable to become non-zero. The sensitivity report in Figure 4.3 includes reduced costs for the two objective function coefficients. A reduced cost tells us how much an objective function coefficient must be improved before the corresponding decision variable gets a value different from zero. In our example, P and Q have values different from zero, and both reduced costs are 0.

The *Objective Coefficient* column provides the current value of the objective coefficient. The next two columns tell how much that coefficient can change before the optimum solution changes. We see that the *Allowable Increase* in the objective coefficient for P is essentially infinity and the *Allowable Decrease* is 15. This means that the unit profit (objective coefficient) can range between 30 and infinity while the current solution (P=100 and Q = 30) remains optimal. The unit profit of Q can range between 0 and 90 with the current solution remaining optimal. It should be emphasized that these ranges are correct only if one profit coefficient is changed at a time.

4.4.3 Find the marginal benefit of increasing the time availability

The part of the sensitivity analysis labeled *Constraints*, gives information concerning changes in the constraint right-hand sides. Each constraint provides a row on this table. The *Cell* entry is the Excel reference to the cell holding the constraint value. The *Name* is provided by the name to the left of the value cell on the model worksheet (column C). The *Final Value* is the amount of the constrained quantity used by the optimum solution. In this case it is the machine time used. The column labeled *Shadow Price* gives the marginal benefits of increasing the time availability. For machines A, C and D the marginal benefit is zero. Since these machines are underutilized, there is obviously no benefit for providing additional minutes.

The shadow price for machine B is 2. This means that an extra minute of machine time yields an increase in profit of $2. This number is valid throughout the range indicated by the last two columns. That is, for product B, the shadow price of 2 is valid for any availability between 1500 and 3000 minutes. Similarly, since the final value of P is equal to the simple upper bound, the shadow price tells us that the objective function will increase by $15 per unit increase of that upper bound (100). That is, for product P, the shadow price of 15 is valid for its demand quantity between 60 and 160 items.

Type of constraint	How does RHS change ?	Is there Slack on constraint ?	How does Z change ?	
			Max Z	Min Z
$\leq$	Up	No	Up	Down
$\leq$	Down	No	Down	Up
$\leq$	Up or down	Yes	No change	No change
$\geq$	Up	No	Down	Up
$\geq$	Down	No	Up	Down
$\geq$	Up or down	Yes	No change	No change

Table 4.1 Changes in Z with changes in the RHS

For constraints shadow prices indicate the impact on Z if the RHS of the constraints are changed. For example in the first constraint which is a $\leq$ constraint representing machine A availability time having zero shadow price, which means that Z will not change with upward(1800 to infinity) changes to the RHS of the first constraint. This follows S1(slack) = 600,which means that we have unused capacity and increasing the time will not change Z.

The explanation of the shadow price for the second constraint is similarly deduced for example the second constraint is a $\leq$ constraint representing Machine B availability, there is no slack on the constraint because S2 (slack) = 0 and it is a maximization problem: Z would go up if the RHS goes up and Z would go down if the RHS goes down. If more time is available Z would go up by $2 for each additional minute of machine availability. If the RHS were reduced by 1 min., Z would go down by $2. But this explanation is valid only if the RHS remains in the 1500 to 3000 range. If the RHS is outside the range. the impact on Z cannot be deduced, and we would have to reformulate the problem again with the new RHS and solve the problem again. For fifth constraint, the explanation of the shadow price can be similarly interpreted for example when the slack is zero then available Z will go up by $15 for each additional product P produced valid only if RHS remains in the 60 to 160 range.

4.4.4 Find the range over which the time availability may change

The *Allowable Increase* and *Decrease* columns give the change in the constraint limit within which the current basis remains optimal. This means the bottlenecks remain the same in this range. We learn from the row for A that the machine availability can go as low as 1800 and as high as infinity. Of course this is reasonable because this constraint is loose with 600 unused minutes for the machine. Similar comments can be made about machines C and D. The range for machine B is from 1500 to 3000 minutes. Since this constraint is tight for the optimum solution, certainly as the time available for B changes, the amounts of products P and Q must change. The interesting result is that the time on machine B and the market for P remain the bottlenecks within the range.

4.5 PARAMETRIC ANALYSIS

In an LP model the coefficients also known as parameters such as i) c_j : profit (cost) contribution per unit of a decision variable, x_j ii) b_i : availability of a resource i, and iii) a_{ij} : consumption of resource i by an unit of a decision variable, x_j are assumed constant and known with certainty during a planning period. However, in real-world situations some data may change over time because of the dynamic nature of the business. Such changes in any of these parameters may raise doubt on the validity of the optimal solution of the given LP model. Thus, decision maker in such situations would like to know how changes in these parameters affect optimal solution and the range within which the optimal solution will remain unchanged with changes in the original input data values. Sensitivity analysis and parametric linear programming are the two techniques that evaluate the relationship between the optimal solution and changes in the LP model parameters.

Sensitivity analysis is the study of knowing the affect on optimal solution of the LP model due to variations in the input coefficients (also called parameters) one at a time, where as parametric analysis is the study of measuring the affect on optimal solution of the LP model due to simultaneous changes in the input coefficients as a function of one parameter. It is simply an extension of sensitivity analysis and aims at finding the various basic solutions that become optimal, one after the other, as the coefficients of the problem change continuously.

The *Vary* button on the worksheet provides a parametric analysis where a single number is varied over a range and the optimum reported for several values.

	A	B	C	D	E	F	G	H	I	J	K
1	Linear Model				Name:	LP_1				Solver:	Excel Solver
2	6300				Type:	LP1				Type:	Linear
3	2		Change		Goal:	Max				Sens.:	Yes
4	TRUE				Profit:	6300				Side:	No
5	TRUE		Solve								
6	TRUE				Variables			1	2		
7	100		Vary		Name:			P	Q		
8	100				Values:			100	30		
9			Change Relation		Lower Bounds:			0	0		
10					Upper Bounds:			100	50		
11											
12					Linear Obj. Coef.:			45	60		
13		Constraints									
14		Num.	Name	Value	Rel.	RHS		Linear Constraint Coefficients			
15		1	MachineA	1800	<=	2400		15	10		
16		2	MachineB	2400	<=	2400		15	30		
17		3	MachineC	1650	<=	2400		15	5		
18		4	MachineD	1150	<=	2400		10	5		
19											

Fig 4.4 Jensen LP Solver spread sheet

4.5.1 Variation in resource availability (Right hand side value)

The time available for machine B is an important parameter, so we vary that value from 0 to 3500 minutes in steps of 500 minutes with the following results. The add-in provides a graph of the objective as a function of the parameter. The limits observed in the sensitivity analysis

42

for the right-hand side of the second constraint are clearly evident in the results.

	Parametric Analysis			Vary: $F$16		Results: $H$8:$I$8
21	Param.	Obj.		P	Q	
22						
23	0	0		0	0	
24	500	1500		33.33333	0	
25	1000	3000		66.66667	0	
26	1500	4500		100	0	
27	2000	5500		100	16.66667	
28	2500	6500		100	33.33333	
29	3000	7500		100	50	
30	3500	7500		100	50	

Table 4.2 Parametric Analysis of RHS of constraint

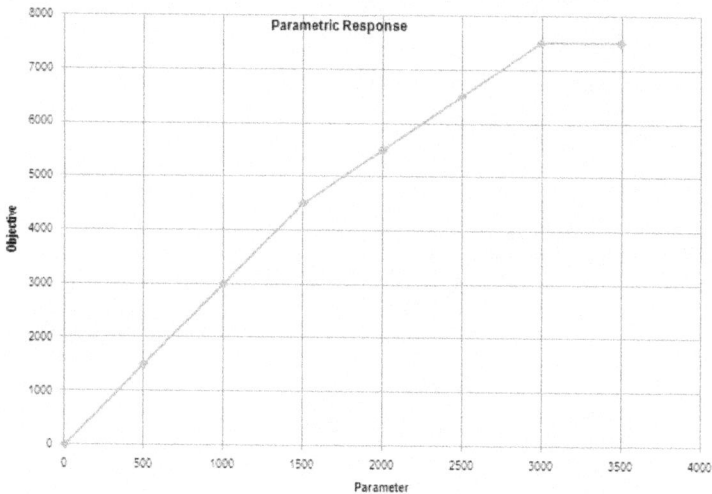

Fig 4.5 Parametric Response of RHS constraint

Below 1500, the variable P is basic, while Q is not. In the range 1500-3000, the variable Q is basic, while P is non-basic at its upper bound. Neither P nor Q is basic above 3000. Both are non-basic variables at their upper bounds.

4.5.2 Variation in resource consumed (coefficient of constraint) per unit of P product

The variation in resource consumed per unit of P product on machine B is an important parameter which can be achieved through some automation, so we vary that value from 0 to

15 minutes in steps of 1.85 minutes with the following results. Below 7.5 min both variables are non-basic at their upper bound. In the range between 7.5-15 variable Q is basic and variable P is non-basic at its upper bound.

	Parametric Analysis	Vary:	$H$16	Results:	$H$8:$I$8
Param.	Obj.	X1	X2		
0	7500	100	50		
1.875	7500	100	50		
3.75	7500	100	50		
5.625	7500	100	50		
7.5	7500	100	50		
9.375	7425	100	48.75		
11.25	7050	100	42.5		
13.125	6675	100	36.25		
15	6300	100	30		

Table 4.3 Parametric analysis of coefficient of variable P

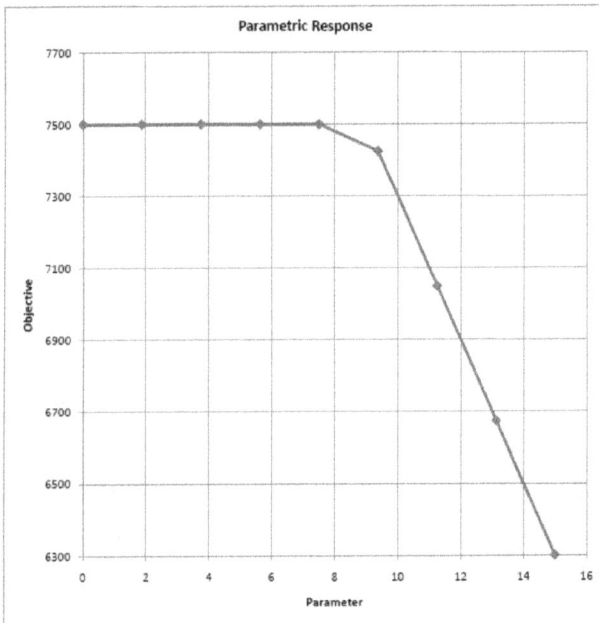

Fig 4.6 Parametric response of coefficient of variable P

44

4.5.3 Variation in resource consumed (coefficient of constraint) per unit of Q product

The variation in resource consumed per unit of Q product on machine B is an important parameter which can be achieved through some automation, so we vary that value from 0 to 30 minutes in steps of 3 minutes with the following results. Below 18 min both variables are non-basic at their upper bound. In the range between 18-30 variable Q is basic and variable P is non-basic at its upper bound.

Param.	Parametric Analysis Obj.	Vary: $I$16 X1	X2	Results: $H$8:$I$8
0	7500	100	50	
3	7500	100	50	
6	7500	100	50	
9	7500	100	50	
12	7500	100	50	
15	7500	100	50	
18	7500	100	50	
21	7071.429	100	42.85714	
24	6750	100	37.5	
27	6500	100	33.33333	
30	6300	100	30	

Table 4.4 Parametric analysis of coefficient of variable Q

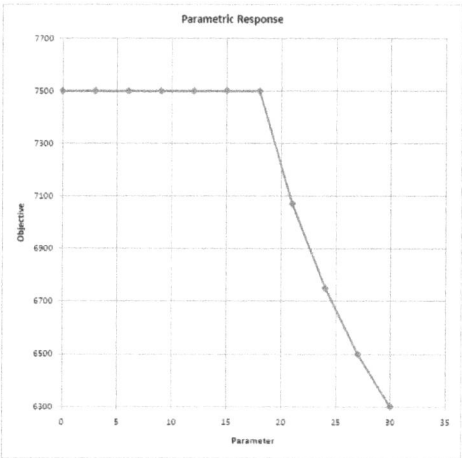

Fig 4.7 Parametric response of coefficient of variable Q

4.6 SUMMARY

In this chapter we carried out sensitivity analysis and identified bottlenecks by interpreting computer solutions which allow us to determine how sensitive the optimal solution is to changes in data values. The Answer report provides the optimal solution of LP problem and gives information about the slack. We studied how does Z change with the changes in RHS of the constraints. We studied the affect on optimal solution as a result of discrete and continuous change in parameters of LP problem. The subsequent chapter summarizes the results of LP problem.

CHAPTER 5
RESULT AND DISCUSSIONS

5.1 INTRODUCTION

This chapter summarizes the results of the LP problem as derived using MATLAB and Excel Solver. Computer software solves problems in mathematical programming by applying different algorithms. For a linear programming problem, a computer would use the simplex method. Firstly, LP product-mix problem was formulated, then the optimal solution that maximizes the profit was found by solving in MATLAB and Excel Solver. The reports generated by computer were interpreted to identify bottlenecks in the manufacturing system and the study of how changes in model parameters affect the optimal solution. In Excel this information is provided in the sensitivity report.

5.2 SEARCH FOR THE OPTIMAL SOLUTION

The optimal solution for the product-mix problem that maximizes profit using MATLAB and Excel Solver is as follows:

Quantity of P products to be manufactured : 100 units/week (Upper Bound)

Quantity of Q products to be manufactured : 30 units/week

Value of Objective Function : $6300/week

Operating Expenses : $ 6000/week

Net Profit : $300/week

The challenge was to find the combination of P and Q within the feasible region that maximizes the objective function (maximizes total profit):

$Z = 45P + 60Q$

Variables	Optimal Value
P	100
Q	30

Table 5.1 Optimum Values

The optimal solution maximizes the objective function and satisfies the given constraints and default constraints: all variables must be greater than or equal to 0.

In this problem we found the (P,Q) that maximizes the objective function and satisfies the constraints of machine A, machine B , machine C, machine D, product P, and product Q as well as the default constraints $P \geq 0$, $Q \geq 0$. The maximum (optimum value of the objective function Z is $6300;the values for (P,Q) that maximizes the objective function and satisfies the constraints is P =100 ,Q = 30.The non-zero P,Q variables are called **basic variables.**

But the optimal solution must be a part of the feasible region At this point we realize that the optimal solution is dependent both on the feasible region and the objective function. When a computer solves a linear programming problem, it starts somewhere in the feasible region and searches for the optimal solution. For our problem, searches will end up in one of the corner points of the feasible region. The particular corner chosen depends on whether the objective function should be maximized or minimized.

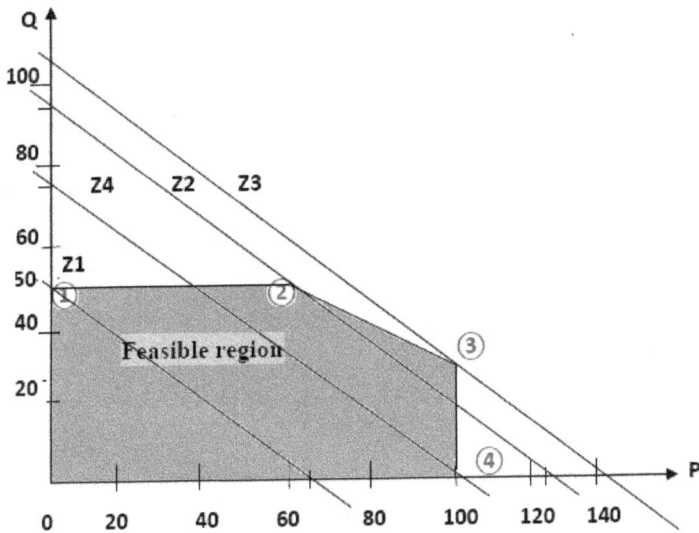

Fig 5.1 Corners of the Feasible Region

$Z1 = 45 \times 0 + 60 \times 50 = \$3000$

$Z2 = 45 \times 60 + 60 \times 50 = \$5700$

$Z3 = 45 \times 100 + 60 \times 30 = \$6300$

$Z4 = 45 \times 100 + 60 \times 0 = \$ 4500$

We can then solve the problem by calculating Z for the corner points of the feasible region (Figure 5.1). The result will still be corner point 3 with $Z = \$6300$.

A higher value of Z gives an objective function line at a higher level as shown for Z3 =$6300 at P=100 and Q= 30. Figure 5.1 shows that as we move the objective function line outwards, the last contact with the feasible region is the corner point made up between the two capacity lines for the machine B and the product P. If the slope of the objective function line changes by putting different values of OFC (unit profit) we may get a new optimal solution. In our problem the slope is $-3/4$: $Q = -3/4P+ Z/60$. (in the form of equation, $y = mx + c$)

The constraints in equations 3.2 and 3.3 tell us that the values of P and Q must lie below all of the capacity lines. These capacity lines, and the constraints P, $Q \geq 0$, define a feasible region shown as the shaded area in Figure 5.1. Combinations of P and Q within the feasible region are the only ones possible. *In this case the feasible region is defined by only three capacity lines (product P, machine B and product Q) and P, $Q \geq 0$.* Note that the machine A, machine C, machine D capacity is not fully used for any combination of P and Q.

5.3 BOTTLENECKS

Bottlenecks happen when a workstation operating at its maximum capacity becomes a bottleneck if the rate of production elsewhere in the plant increases but throughput at that workstation cannot be increased to meet demand. Clearly from Fig 4.3 the time on machine B is a bottleneck for this situation. The market for P is also a bottleneck because the optimum value is the upper bound for P. If either the time on machine B or the market for product P are increased, the profit will increase

5.4 RANGE OVER WHICH THE UNIT PROFIT MAY CHANGE

The *Objective Coefficient* column in Fig 4.3 provides the current value of the objective coefficient. The next two columns tell how much that coefficient can change before the optimum solution changes. We see that the *Allowable Increase* in the objective coefficient for P is essentially infinity and the *Allowable Decrease* is 15. This means that the unit profit (objective coefficient) can range between 30 and infinity while the current solution (P=100 and Q = 30) remains optimal. The unit profit of Q can range between 0 and 90 with the current solution remaining optimal.

It should be emphasized that these ranges are correct only if one profit coefficient is changed at a time.

OFC of variables	Allowable increase	Allowable decrease	Coefficient (C)
C (P)	INF	15	45
C (Q)	30	60	60

Table 5.2 Range of Objective Function Coefficients

The table 5.2 shows the range of the Objective Function Coefficients that maintains the current value of the solution: any coefficient change that is greater or less than these values will change the value of the optimum solution variables. Note that if the changes are outside of these ranges then we must re-solve the problem.

In this problem, suppose the coefficient of variable Q changes from 60 to 80. We expect the current basic solution set (P,Q) and values to be the same since the allowable interval is [60-60,60+30].When we solve the problem, the new optimal solution will be P=100,Q=30,hence the basic variable set and values are still the same. Note that the value of the objective function changes due to changed coefficient.

Suppose the coefficient of variable Q changes from 60 to 100.We expect the current basic solution set (P,Q) and values to be different since the allowable interval is [60-60,60+30].When we re-solve the problem, the new optimal solution is different including basic variable set and values. and the value of objective function is changed.

5.5 MARGINAL BENEFIT OF INCREASING THE TIME AVAILABILITY

The column labeled *Shadow Price in Fig 4.3* gives the marginal benefits of increasing the time availability. For machines A, C and D the marginal benefit is zero. Since these machines are under -utilized, there is obviously no benefit for providing additional minutes.

The shadow price for machine B is 2. This means that an extra minute of machine time yields increase in profit of $2. This number is valid throughout the range indicated by the last two columns. That is, for machine B, the shadow price of 2 is valid for any availability between 1500 and 3000 minutes.

Constraint	Shadow Price	Constraint RHS	Allowable increase	Allowable decrease
Machine B	2	2400	600	900
Market P	15	100	60	40

Table 5.3 Shadow Prices for Constraints

The shadow prices are the objective function coefficients for the slack or surplus variables at the optimum solution. The rate that the objective changes if the Right Hand Side of a constraint is changed. Shadow prices are also called Lagrange multipliers. For each constraint, the shadow price tells how much the objective function will change if we change the Right Hand Side of the constraint within the allowable increase and decrease limits.

The Shadow Price = Change in optimal objective function value per unit increase of a corresponding RHS coefficient.

In this problem, if you change the RHS of constraint machine B from 2400 to 2500 and re-solve the problem we expect that the objective function currently valued at 6300 to increase (by 100* shadow price = 100*2=200) to 6500. In fact, in this case, the new optimal solution will be different.

5.6 RANGE OVER WHICH THE TIME AVAILABILITY MAY CHANGE

The *Allowable Increase* and *Decrease* columns in Fig 4.3 give the change in the constraint limit within which the current basis remains optimal. This means the bottlenecks remain the same in this range. We learn from the row for machine A that the machine availability can go as low as 1800 and as high as infinity. Of course this is reasonable because this constraint is loose with 600 unused minutes for the machine. Similar comments can be made about machines C and D.

The range for machine B is from 1500 to 3000 minutes. Since this constraint is tight for the optimum solution, certainly as the time available for B changes, the amounts of products P and Q must change. The interesting result is that the time on machine B and the market for P remain the bottlenecks within the range.

Constraint	Allowable increase	Allowable decrease	RHS coefficient
Machine A	INF	600	2400
Machine B	600	900	2400
Machine C	INF	750	2400
Machine D	INF	1250	2400
Market P	60	40	100
Market Q	INF	20	50

Table 5.4 Range of RHS Coefficients

The table 5.4 shows the range of the RHS coefficients that maintains current basic solution variables: any RHS change that is greater or less than these values will change the non-zero (basic) variable set. Note that the values of the basic variables will change.

In this problem, suppose the RHS coefficient of machine B changes from 2400 to 2500.We expect the current basic solution set (P,Q) to be the same since the allowable interval is [2400-900, 2400+600].When we re-solve the problem, the new optimal solution will be different but the basic variable set will be the same (P,Q).

If the RHS coefficient of machine B changes from2400 to 3100, expect the current basic solution set to be different since the RHS coefficient is outside the allowable interval [2400-900, 2400+600].When we re-solve the problem, the new optimal solution will be different.

5.7 REDUCED COST FOR NON-BASIC VARIABLES

The reduced costs are the objective function coefficients for the original variables at the optimum solution. It is an estimate of how much function will change if you make a zero-valued variable non-zero. If it has −ve sign then the objective function value will increase and if + ve sign then the objective function value will decrease. Reduced cost is the amount by which the OFC for the variable needs to change before that variable becomes non-zero. Reduced costs are also called reduced gradients and opportunity coats.

The reduced costs = Change in optimal objective function value per unit increase of a corresponding variable currently at a value of zero.

For example if P had been zero-valued variable then we would have got some reduced cost say -15.Suppose we make new constraint : P = 2.This increases P from 0 to 2. When we re-solve the problem we expect that the objective function currently valued at 6300 will increase (by 2* reduced cost = 2*15 =30) to 6330.In fact, in this case the new optimal solution will be different.

In this problem the reduced costs are zero because optimal solution consists of all non-zero variables.

5.8 SLACK VALUES FOR CONSTRAINTS

The slack variable is a variable that converts an inequality to an equality. In this problem, note that the constraints for machine B and market P are satisfied exactly : For P = 100 and Q = 30 we see

Constraint	Slack value
Machine A	600
Machine C	750
Machine D	1250
Market Q	20

Table 5.5 Slack values for constraints

Machine B : $15*100 + 30* 30 = 2400 = 2400$

Market P   : $1*100 = 100$

In these cases the slack variables for constraints are zero.

Note that constraints for machine A, machine C, machine D and market Q are not satisfied exactly.: For P = 100 and Q = 30 we see

Machine A : $15*100 + 10*30 = 1800 \leq 2400$

In this case the value of the slack variable is 600. Similarly, it can be found for other constraints.

5.9 RECOMMENDED COURSE OF ACTION

5.9.1 Product Outsourcing

Manufacturing often function in situation where internal production resources constrain their throughput. Such situations are characterized by market demand in excess of the company's production capacity. Management policy is to meet all demand in order to prevent competitor from entering the arena .Now if management needs to decide what quantities of each product to manufacture and what quantities to buy from external contractors.

For this we continue with our LP analysis and the methodology is described as follows. Let contractor supply P product for $ 60 and Q product for $ 65. These prices include the cost of raw materials.

		PRODUCT P	PRODUCT Q
1	Market price per unit	$ 90	$ 100
2	Raw material cost per unit	$ 45	$ 40
3	Throughput/unit	$ 45	$ 60
4	Demand in units	100	50
5	Units to manufacture	100	30
6	Throughput/ manufactured unit	$ 45	$ 60
7	Units contracted outside	0	20
8	Throughput/contracted unit	$ 30	$ 35
9	Total product throughput	$ 4500	1800 + 700 = $ 2500
10	Total facility throughput	$ 7000	
11	Operating expenses	$ 6000	
12	Net Profit	$ 1000	

Table 5.6 Product Outsourcing data

We proceed to compute the throughput of the product mix solution. The throughput of each manufactured unit is the market price less cost of raw materials. The figure is multiplied by the number of units manufactured. The throughput of each unit contracted outside is computed as its market price less the price paid to the contractor. Total product throughput is the sum of it manufactured and contracted throughputs. From the total facility throughput of $ 7000 we subtract its operating expenses of $ 6000 generating a net profit of $ 1000.

5.9.2 One-time cost

If we calculate one- time cost with $Z = 45 P + 60 Q$ subject to $55 P + 50 Q \leq 9600$, $P \geq 100$, $Q \geq 50$, then on solving with the help of Excel Solver we obtain $P = 100$, $Q = 82$ and $Z = \$ 9420$ as shown in figure 5.2.

	A	B	C	D	E	F	G
1	Microsoft Excel 12.0 Answer Report						
2	Worksheet: [Book1]Sheet1						
3	Report Created: 8/14/2013 11:34:02 PM						
4							
5							
6	Target Cell (Max)						
7		Cell	Name	Original Value	Final Value		
8		$H$4	z	9420	9420		
9							
10							
11	Adjustable Cells						
12		Cell	Name	Original Value	Final Value		
13		$B$4		100	100		
14		$C$4		82	82		
15							
16							
17	Constraints						
18		Cell	Name	Cell Value	Formula	Status	Slack
19		$D$7		9600	$D$7<=$F$7	Binding	0
20		$D$8		100	$D$8>=$F$8	Binding	0
21		$D$9		82	$D$9>=$F$9	Not Binding	32
22							

Fig 5.2 Answer Report of One-Time cost

5.9.3 Cross training of one machine operator

If we try with one operator of machine D trained to operate machine B for 600 min. then without paying overtime time to machine B operator then we can achieve max Z = $7500 for P = 100 and Q = 50.

5.9.4 Possibility of third product manufacturing

If third hypothetical product R is manufactured with a throughput of $5/unit and maximum market demand to be 100 with processing time of 1 min each on under- utilized machines A, C and D then on solving on MATLAB we get the following results.

Machine A is utilized for 1900 min, machine B for 2400 min, machine C for 1750 min. and machine D for 1250 min. The optimal solution will be P =100, Q =30, R = 100 and Z value is $6800. If processing time is increased to 6 min each on machines A,C and D then machine A is fully utilized for 2400 min, machine C for 2250 min and machine D for 1750 min. with optimal solution unchanged.

Command Format for solving P, Q, R problem in MATLAB

Max Z = 45P + 60Q + 5R

Subject to:

$15P + 10Q + R \leq 2400$

$15P + 30Q \quad\ \leq 2400$

$15P + \ 5Q + R \leq 2400$

$10P + \ 5Q + R \leq 2400$

$P \qquad\qquad \leq \quad 100$

$\qquad Q \qquad \leq \quad 50$

$\qquad\qquad R \leq \quad 100$

$\qquad P, Q, R \ \geq \quad 0$

The above LP formulation is converted into following format for solving in MATLAB:

Max $Z = f x$ or min $Z = -f x$

$\qquad$ s.t $\ A x \leq b$

$\qquad\qquad$ Aeq = beq

$\qquad\qquad$ $x \geq l x$

$\qquad\qquad$ $\leq u$

Now, using the command formats we solve the problem as follows:

$x = \text{linprog} (f, A, b, Aeq, beq, l, u)$

$$f = - \begin{bmatrix} 45 \\ 60 \\ 5 \end{bmatrix} \qquad\qquad A = \begin{bmatrix} 15 & 10 & 1 \\ 15 & 30 & 0 \\ 15 & 5 & 1 \\ 10 & 5 & 1 \end{bmatrix}$$

$$b = \begin{bmatrix} 2400 \\ 2400 \\ 2400 \\ 2400 \end{bmatrix} \qquad\qquad Aeq = [\ ] \qquad\qquad beq = [\ ]$$

$$l = \begin{bmatrix} 0 \\ 0 \\ 0 \end{bmatrix} \qquad\qquad u = \begin{bmatrix} 100 \\ 50 \\ 100 \end{bmatrix}$$

Input the variables into MATLAB we get

>> f = - [45 ; 60 ; 5] ;

>> A = [15 10 1 ; 15 30 0 ; 15 5 1 ; 10 5 1] ;

>> b = [2400 ; 2400 ; 2400 ; 2400] ;

>> Aeq = [ ] ;

>> beq = [ ] ;

>> l = [0 ; 0 ; 0] ;

>> u = [100 ; 50 ; 100] ;

>> x = linprog (f, A, b, Aeq, beq, l, u)

Solve the problem using MATLAB and we get the following results

P = 100, Q = 30 and R = 100

5.9.5 Optimal Sequencing to process jobs on machines

As discussed in chapter 3 about the sequencing problem of processing two jobs through four machines, the total minimum elapsed time including idle time is 60 min. for both jobs 1 and 2. It means both products P and Q will take 60 min to complete on all four machines with the optimal sequence. Thus, in 9600 min. of total available time per week on all 4 machines we can manufacture maximum quantity 160 units of both products provided all machines are 100 percent utilized. But due to difference in processing times and continuous production flow there will be bottlenecks at machine B since it is engaged for more time than machines A, C and D. Hence, due to these constraints actual quantity 130 units can be manufactured with optimal solution of P=100 and Q=30 as derived through MATLAB and Excel Solver.

5.10 SUMMARY

One of the common types of Linear Programming problems encountered by the operations managers is product mix which may be of direct strategic importance because they can be integral to the development of long run business strategy . How best to allocate these scarce resources can only be determined with the use of Linear Programming. We studied the LP problem with two variables and six constraints and solved it with the help of MATLAB and Excel Solver and finally got satisfactory results. In addition to an optimal solution, Solver can produce a sensitivity report with valuable information about a linear programming model.

The simplex method is the most common type analytic tool for solving LP models. Although use of the simplex method by hand to solve LPs is tedious and error prone, hence real LP problems are always solved on computers. With the help of parametric analysis we studied the affect of continuous change in parameters on the optimal solution. The optimal sequencing to process the two jobs on four machines was determined.

CHAPTER 6
CONCLUSIONS

6.1 INTRODUCTION

Our main focus of the study was how best to allocate the limited resources with the use of Linear Programming model. Resource scarcities can cause hectic shifts in operations strategies to meet objectives; additionally, many resources prices are skyrocketing. The limited quantity of resources available and their high prices act as a double-barreled incentive to use them to the greatest advantage. Today, perhaps as never before, operations mangers understand that operations strategies must be accomplished within constraints imposed on their organizations by the shortage of resources. Operations researchers possess the knowledge and skills to analyze business problems and apply different quantitative tools to improve situations. They use a variety of computer packages in these efforts.

One of the ways that operations managers determine how best to allocate their scarce resources is with the use of Linear Programming (LP). Hence, we come to the following conclusions that:

- A problem where all decision variables are linearly related can be solved using linear programming.
- A linear programming model with two decision variables can be solved graphically.
- MATLAB software and Excel's Solver are an appropriate tool to solve linear programming models.
- In addition to an optimal solution, Solver can produce a sensitivity report with valuable information about a linear programming model.
- It highlights the bottlenecks in the production processes which is one of the most significant advantages of linear programming.

6.2 SUMMARY OF THE PRESENT WORK

A Linear Programming problem of Product mix having two variables and six constraints was solved for its optimal solution using MATLAB software. The sensitivity analysis was done with the help of reports generated by Excel Solver. The Answer report provides the optimal solution of LP problem and gives information about the Slack variables which represent the amount of unused/unutilized resources. Sensitivity report provides reduced costs which represents the amount by which OFC of a particular decision variable should increase to change the value of decision variable from 0 to 1 , shadow prices indicate the impact on Z if the RHS of the constraints are changed and sensitivity ranges for the variables and the constraint bounds. The parametric analysis done to study the affect of continuous change in parameters on the optimal solution. Also, using graphical method the optimal scheduling has been determined to process two jobs on four machines and calculated total elapsed time to complete the two jobs.

6.3 SUMMARY OF CONTRIBUTIONS

As an analyst the search for an optimal solution of LP problem was achieved. The final results as derived using the computer softwares MATLAB and Excel Solver were interpreted and applied to support strategic management decisions of the company. In my present study a method has been worked out to solve a product-mix problem and explained how best to approach the constrained decisions of strategic importance to the manufacturer using latest versions of computer softwares. Hence, this thesis work demonstrates the use of powerful linear programming and other analysis tools to solve complex, constrained business problems.

6.4 SCOPE FOR FUTURE WORK

The extensions of this study would be to identify bottlenecks and sensitivity analysis using **Fuzzy Algorithm** which allows us to determine how sensitive the optimal solution is to changes in data values. This includes analyzing changes in :

i) An Objective Function Coefficient (OFC)

ii) A Right Hand Side (RHS) value of a constraint.

6.5 CONCLUDING REMARKS

The present work demonstrates the successful application oriented effort on solving Linear Programming model of Product-Mix using computer softwares. The demonstration of application of quantitative methods and techniques to business problems and to support strategic management decisions in order to best utilize a company's resources and making the most of limited resources like operating expenses, machine capacity, market constraints should be a motivation for organizations to focus on improving operations and reducing costs for its survival in a highly competitive industry.

REFERENCES

1. Al-Shammari, Minwir, and Isaam Dawood. *–Linear Programming Applied to a Production Blending Problem :A spread sheet Modelling Approach.*‖Production & Inventory Management Journal 38,no.1 (1997):1-7.

2. Ambs,Ken,Sebastian Cwilich,Mei Deng, and David J.Houck.‖*Optimizing Restoration Capacity in the AT&T Network.*‖Interfaces 30,no.1 (2000):26-44.

3. Anderson, David R.,Dennis J. Sweeney, and Thomas A.Williams. *An Introduction to Management Science: Quantitive Approaches to Decision Making,*9th ed.Cincinnati,OH:South-Western College Publishing,2000.

4. Anderson Randy I, Robert Fok, and John Scott.‖*Hotel Industry Efficiency: An Advanced Linear Programming Examination.*‖ American Business Review 18,no.1 (January 2000):40-48

5.Camm,Jeff,and James R.Evans. *Management Science and Decision Technology.*Cincinnati,OH: South-Western College Publishing,2000.

6. Chakarvarti, Nilotpal. *Tea Company Steeped in OR.* OR/MS Today, no. 2 (April 2000):32-34.

7. Flt Lt Dinesh Kumar Gupta. *Linear Programming in MATLAB'* International Journal of Industrial Engineering Research and Development. (IJIERD), ISSN 0976-6979, www.iaeme.com/ijierd.asp, vol.4, issue1, pp 19-24, Jan- Apr 2013.

8.Guven, S., and E. Persentili. *A Linear Programming Model for Bank Balance Sheet Management.* Omega 25, no. 4 (August 1997): 449-459

9. Hillier, Frederick S,and Gerald J. Liebermann.*Introduction to Operations Research.* New York: Mcgraw-Hill,2001.

10.Kolman,Bernard, and Robert E.Beck. *Elementary Linear Programming with Applications.*2nd ed.San Diego:Academic Press,1995.

11.Moore,Jeffrey H.,and Larry R. Weatherford. *Decision Modeling with Microsoft Excel,*6thed.Upper Saddle River,NJ: Prentice Hill,2001.

12. O.S. Balogun, E.T. Jolayemi, T.J. Akingbade, H.G. Muazu . *Use Of Linear Programming For Optimal Production In A Production Line In Coca –Cola Bottling Company, Ilorin,* International Journal of Engineering Research and Applications (IJERA) ISSN: 2248-9622 www.ijera.com Vol. 2, Issue 5, September- October 2012, pp.2004-2007.

13. Ragsdale, Cliff. *Spreadsheet Modeling And Decision Analysis,* 3rd ed. Cincinnati, OH: South-Western College Publishing, 2001.

14. ShowSimplex, Linear Optimization, 2002, Inductive Solutions.Inc

15.Vanderbei, Robert J. – Linear Programming: A modern Integrated Analysis‖. *Interfaces* 27, no.2 (March-April 1997):120-122.